Counting from Creation

For my darlings Ella, Colby, Elysa, and Emily. You are my inspiration to write, play, and most importantly, draw closer to God. I love you more than you could ever imagine.
T.W.

For my angels here—Chuck, Brody, and Blaine— and my angel there, my mom.
A.S.

Counting from Creation
Copyright © 2013 by Tracy Wainwright for text
Copyright © 2013 by Angie Satterfield for illustrations

All rights reserved. No portion of this book may be reproduced or transmitted in any form or by any means, electronic or mechanical, including photocopying and recording, or by any information storage and retrieval system, without permission in writing from the publisher, except for brief excerpts in reviews.

ISBN-13: 978-0989948524
ISBN-10: 0989948528

TLC Wainwright Publishing, LLC

Counting from Creation

Tracy Wainwright
illustrated by Angie Satterfield

tlc

TLC Wainwright Publishing, LLC
VA

One God, perfect, holy and good
since even before the beginning;
In His image He created man and woman,
He cared for them and warned about sinning.

Yet still they shunned and scorned His care,
His love, His affection;
Through choosing wrong, picking sin,
they stepped out of His protection.

Two people, devoted to God,
  being still, hearkening their ear;
Listening, choosing to obey,
  when His angel did appear.

Mary and Joseph, dedicated and faithful to the Creator; Waited patiently, trusting, **obeying** the Lord, the great vindicator.

Three gifts, carried by Magi,
  given to a wee little king;
The gents unnumbered traveled afar,
  priceless, precious presents to bring.

The first to bow, to bend the knee,
    to acknowledge His wondrous glory
Taking part in the dawning
    of the most **breathtaking** story.

Four hundred years of waiting long,
God's chosen people without a word;
Had watched expectantly for their **Messiah**,
Who in a babe's cry was heard.

Many distracted, went their own way,
others longingly waited;
Some recognized the Word become flesh,
and boldly and bravely stated.

Five small loaves, generously given
from a boy so innocent and young;
An example of **authentic love**,
shown in action, not only in tongue.

In the hands of God's Chosen One,

His Deliverer, His only Son;

He proved anything, by the power

of the Holy Spirit, can be done.

Six days, God selected and used,
to fashion a world out of naught;
Forming birds, lizards, and lilies,
all of creation with just a thought.

Jesus, even from creation promised,
during His life on earth proclaimed;
No work on the seventh day, but rest,
and He called it the **Sabbath**, as it was named.

Seven times is **not near enough**,
  the mighty Son of God declared;
    To pardon an offense, a hurt,
      when it feels like no one has cared.

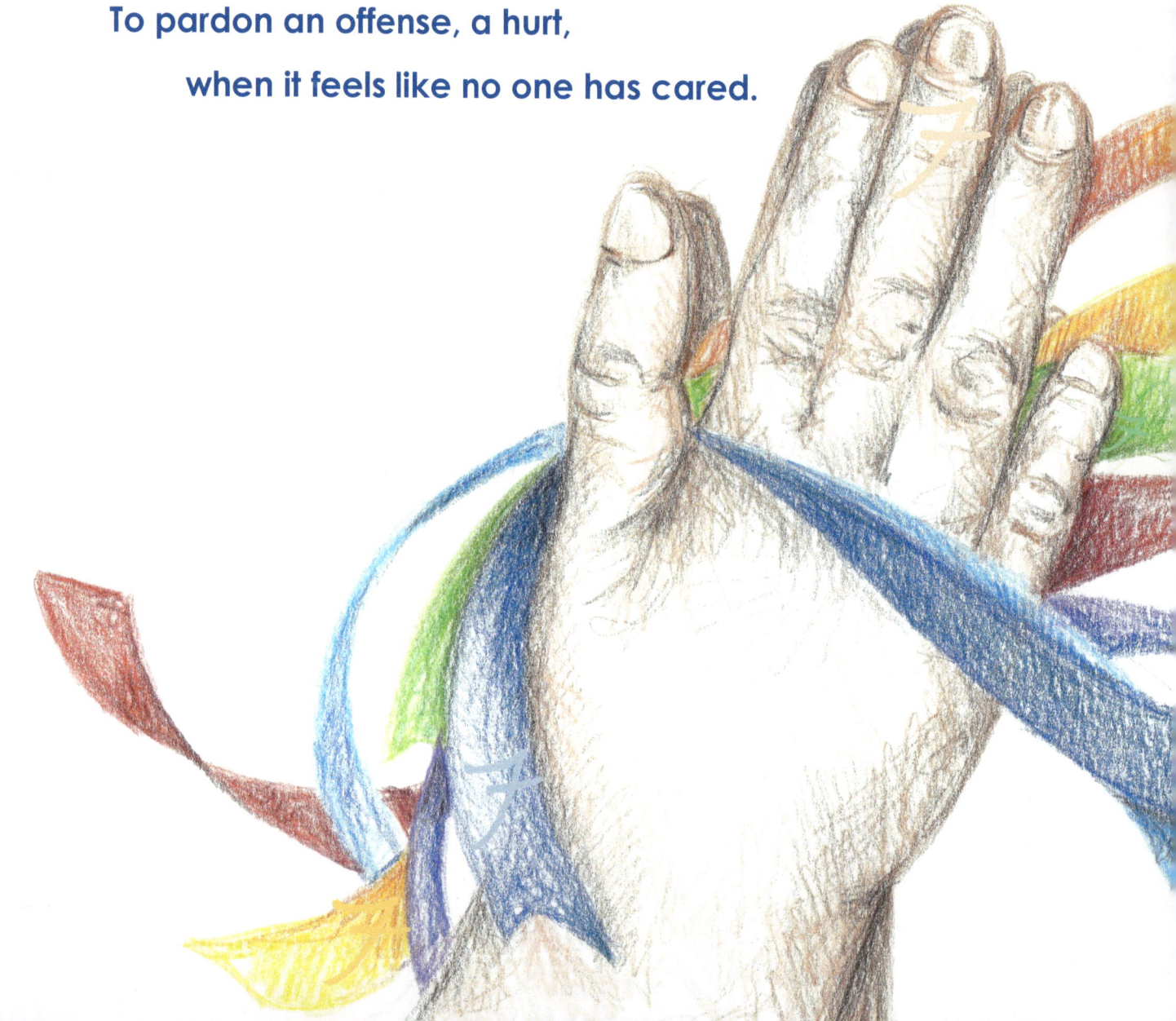

Seventy times seven,
   too many to count,
      we are to forgive;
Following our Heavenly Father,
   under whose grace we live.

Eight days after
  Jesus shared his heart
about His death
  He knew would come;
He called men
  to follow after Him,
to give up all
  and not just some.

He went up
 a mountain to pray;
  and became as brilliant
   as pure light.
The Father saying,
 "Listen to my Son;"
  Revealing His glory,
   power, and might.

Nine men happy with the healing,
never came to gratitude express;
Only one returned praising God,
his gratefulness to
loudly profess.

An example is he for us,
    always remembering to give thanks;
Lest we forget, grumble and complain,
    thus becoming all around cranks.

Ten commandments, laws given,
to shelter us in the Most High;
Aimed to **guide** our **hearts** to the Lord,
who calls us the apple of His eye.

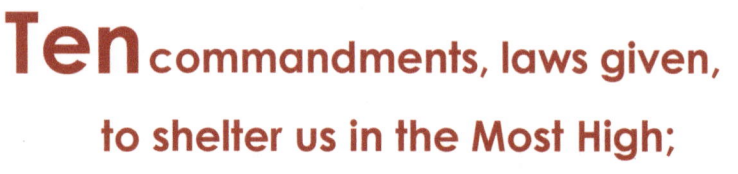

Ten was the number, Jesus affirmed,
    yet summed up in the greatest two.
Love God with everything we have;
    love others also, living what is true.

Eleven disciples stayed loyal, dedicated to the end; When Jesus died for every trespass and showed the greatest love for a friend.

Eleven rejoicing, that He,
the crucified Christ,
to life again arose;
Death overcome,
the Good News spreading,
His mercy and
grace to expose.

Twelve sons, tribes of the chosen,
and twelve apostles of the Lamb;
God's people given the Word, the Truth,
the promise of the Great I am.

Faithful, compassionate,
    to life everlasting He'll always beckon;
Glory revealed, forgiveness offered,
    desiring us forever in heaven.

Numbers with scripture references each poem is based on

One God, perfect, holy, and good, since even before the beginning;
In His image He created man and woman, He cared for them and warned them about sinning.
Yet still they shunned and scorned His care, His love, His affection;
Through choosing wrong, picking sin, they stepped out of His protection.
Genesis 1:1; Genesis 1:27; Genesis 3:1-6

Two people, devoted to God, being still, hearkening their ear;
Listening, choosing to obey, when His angel did appear.
Mary and Joseph, dedicated and faithful to the Creator;
Waited patiently, trusting, obeying the Lord, the great vindicator.
Luke 1:28-33; Matthew 1:20-24

Three gifts, carried by Magi, given to a wee little king;
The gents unnumbered traveled afar, priceless, precious presents to bring.
The first to bow, to bend the knee, to acknowledge His wondrous glory;
Taking part in the dawning of the most breathtaking story.
Matthew 2:1-2, 11

Four hundred years of waiting long, God's chosen people without a word;
Had watched expectantly for their Messiah, who in a babe's cry was heard.
Many distracted, went their own way, others longingly waited;
Some recognized the Word become flesh, and boldly and bravely stated.
Luke 2:25-32; Luke 2:36-38; John 1:1-4, 14

Five small loaves, generously given from a boy so innocent and young;
An example of authentic love, shown in action, not only in tongue.
In the hands of God's Chosen One, His Deliverer, His only Son;
He proved anything, by the power of the Holy Spirit, can be done.
John 6:9-13

Six days, God selected and used, to fashion a world out of naught;
Forming birds, lizards, and lilies, all of creation with just a thought.
Jesus, even from creation promised, during His life on earth proclaimed;
No work on the seventh day, but rest. and He called it the Sabbath, as it was named.
Genesis 1:1-2:3; Genesis 3:14-15; Luke 6:5

Make sure you count the items on each page!

Seven times is not near enough, the mighty Son of God declared;
To pardon an offense, a hurt, or when it feels like no one has cared.
Seventy-seven times, too many to count, we are to forgive;
Following our Heavenly Father, whose grace under which we live.
Matthew 18:21-22

Eight days after Jesus shared his heart about His death He knew would come;
Calling men to follow after Him, to give up all and not just some.
He went up a mountain to pray; and became as brilliant as pure light.
The Father saying, "Listen to my Son;" Revealing His glory, power, and might.
Luke 9:23-36

Nine men happy with the healing, never came to gratitude express;
Only one returned praising God, his gratefulness to loudly profess.
An example is he for us, always remembering to give thanks;
Lest we forget, grumble, and complain, thus becoming all around cranks.
Luke 17:11-19; Ephesians 5:20; Philippians 4:4-6

Ten Commandments, laws given, to shelter us in the Most High;
Aimed to guide our hearts to the Lord, who calls us the apple of His eye.
Ten was the number, Jesus affirmed, yet summed up in the greatest two.
Love God with everything we have; Love others also, living what is true.
Exodus 20:1-17; Matthew 22:35-40

Eleven disciples stayed loyal, dedicated to the end;
When Jesus died for every trespass and showed the greatest love of a friend.
Eleven rejoicing, that He, the crucified Christ, to life again arose;
Death overcome, the Good News spreading, His mercy and grace to expose.
Acts 2:14, 29-36, 38

Twelve sons, twelve tribes of the chosen, and twelve apostles of the Lamb;
God's people given the Word, the Truth, the promise of the Great I Am.
Faithful, compassionate, to life everlasting He'll always beckon;
Glory revealed, forgiveness offered, desiring us forever in heaven.
Genesis 35:22b; John 3:16; John 14:6; Acts 7:8; Romans 3:1-4; Revelation 21:12

Did you find all of the numbers on each page set? There is the same number of each number hidden in the picture on each page set. (One 1, two 2s, three 3s, etc.)

www.ingramcontent.com/pod-product-compliance
Lightning Source LLC
LaVergne TN
LVHW071028070426
835507LV00002B/70